Real Estate Financing

Strategies for Structuring Debt and Equity

Jeffrey S. Loomis

Copyright

Table of Contents

Dedication

In profound gratitude to the Almighty God, the unwavering pillar of strength and guidance throughout this journey. To my cherished family, whose unwavering support and understanding have been my foundation, I extend my deepest appreciation.

To the visionary real estate investors who dare to dream and build, this book is dedicated to you. Your resilience, creativity, and commitment to shaping the future of our built environment inspire every word on these pages.

With heartfelt **thanks**,

Jeffrey S Loomis

Author Bio

Loomis is Known for his innovative leadership and significant influence on the real estate sector, Jeffrey S. Loomis is a renowned figure in the field. Throughout the course of his remarkable career spanning many decades, Loomis has established himself as a creative force and strategic thinker in the real estate development industry.

As an experienced real estate agent, Loomis has handled a variety of markets with skill, with a deep awareness of market trends and a remarkable capacity to turn obstacles into opportunities. In addition to contributing to his success, his dedication to eco-friendly and progressive methods has sparked a fresh wave of ecologically aware real estate development.

Loomis's accomplishments are felt in the communities he has impacted, not only in boardrooms and designs. His works serve as living examples of his dedication to perfection, transforming skylines and improving the lives of those who occupy his painstakingly designed settings.

Jeffrey S. Loomis is a thought leader, mentor, and positive change agent who continues to influence real estate history and leave a lasting legacy that goes far beyond the structures he builds.

Introduction

Welcome to an educational voyage written by Jeffrey S. Loomis. Through the prism of sustainable development, we will examine the complex web of equity partnerships, strategic exits, and real estate finance in the pages that follow.

As we set out on our journey, picture a path lighted by Loomis's vast real estate experience. Discover the subtleties of executing a smooth departure, the artistry of designing equity partnerships, and the critical role that green finance plays in establishing a sustainable future.

This book serves as a guide for both seasoned real estate professionals and aspiring enthusiasts, offering more than simply a compilation of insightful information. Readers may get a deep grasp of market dynamics, creative funding structures, and the strategic acumen needed to manage the always-changing terrain by embracing the advice contained inside.

For those who delve inside these pages, there are several advantages.

Anticipate discovering

★ **Strategic Mastery**

Use a seasoned industry expert's strategic insights to navigate the complexities of real estate with grace.

★ **Innovative finance Knowledge**

Understand the nuances of equity partnerships, sustainable practices, and green finance, which redefine success in the real estate industry.

★ **Inspiring Judgment**

Discover the secrets of profitable exits and equity arrangements, which will enable you to make wise and creative judgments about your real estate endeavors.

★ Sustainability Integration

Acquire the skills necessary to incorporate sustainability into your projects, not just for the benefit of the environment but also as a competitive advantage in the real estate market.

Join Jeffrey S. Loomis as he takes you on a transforming trip where you will learn to imagine, plan, and create in the fast-paced real estate industry.

Chapter 1

What Exactly Is Real Estate Finance

To achieve success in real estate finance,it is essential to have a basic understanding of the subject matter. This is true regardless of whether you want to purchase a home or invest in commercial property. Real estate finance is a subject of labor that is both exciting and hard. *It involves the planning, management, and analysis of financial resources that are related to residential and commercial loans and buildings.* Within the scope of this chapter, an introduction is provided to several significant topics and concepts, such as real estate finance occupations and valuation methodologies of various kinds.

What You Need to Know About Real Estate Finance Fundamentals

Real estate finance is a discipline that focuses on how individuals acquire real estate, whether it be a home, an office building, or a piece of land. It includes the analysis, planning, and management of financial resources related to real estate, commercial loans, and properties. Some of the things that go under this area include commercial loans and properties. Additionally, it encompasses financial operations that are associated with real estate, such as the acquisition, development, construction, and management of residential and commercial real estate developments. As can be seen, the field of finance encompasses a vast variety of subjects. Let's take a more in-depth look at the many types of real estate as well as the roles in real estate finance that finance professionals might be interested in working in.

Varieties of Real Estate

Real estate may be classified into two basic categories: residential and commercial. Although there are some similarities between the two categories of attributes, they are also completely distinct from one another.

Business Property

Assets that are largely employed for business purposes are referred to as commercial real estate.

Examples of such assets include retail outlets, office buildings, **warehouses, industrial structures, and land designated for commercial use**. Businesses, real estate brokers, investors, or developers frequently own commercial premises, which they subsequently lease or rent to tenants.Commercial properties can be valued in several ways, including the capitalization rate, Gross Rent Multiplier (GRM), sales comparisons (comps), replacement rates, or the market. Of these methods, the capitalization rate, or the value determined by the property's potential for profit, is often used in valuing.In this method, the value is determined by the net operating income (NOI), This is the yearly revenue less the costs of the property. The property is seen to be more valuable the higher the NOI.

Given that they are frequently more expensive than residential dwellings, commercial structures demand a substantial initial investment. To acquire or construct commercial buildings, real estate owners and developers typically need to secure money for their projects.

Household Property

Properties employed for residential purposes, such as townhouses, apartments, condos, and single-family homes, are referred to as residential real estate. Usually, owners of residential properties are persons or families who either use the property themselves or rent it out to renters.

*There are **three** basic ways used to evaluate residential properties:* **fair market value, appraised value, and assessed value.** Each approach has a distinct function. For instance, a home's price to prospective buyers is decided by its

16

fair market value.It analyzes the property's size, location, amenities, and general condition to other similar homes in the neighborhood. The assessed value, which is commonly applied when refinancing or purchasing a house via a loan, must be evaluated by a professional appraiser. The local county tax assessor calculates the assessed value to collect the appropriate amount of property taxes. Due to their comparatively lower cost compared to commercial structures, residential real estate is more accessible for individual investors. Nevertheless, whether someone chooses to purchase a house or rent will rely on their financial status and available real estate finance possibilities. Since the normal person is generally not educated about every facet of the house-buying procedure, they look to real estate finance professionals with expertise for guidance.

Real Estate Finance Careers

When it comes to aiding individuals and firms in acquiring loans or other sorts of real estate financing from banks, mortgage lenders, or other financial institutions, real estate finance professionals are vital. A degree in finance, real estate, or a related area is typically essential for work in this sector, in addition to appropriate experience and industry certifications.

Professionals in real estate finance generally require the following talents to succeed

★ **Mapping finances**

★ **Underwriting and valuation**

★ **Knowledge of capital markets**

★ Analytics for the real estate market

Let's review a couple of the opportunities that are accessible in real estate finance.

Analyst for Real Estate

A real estate analyst analyzes information and builds financial models to aid in directing investment decisions based on market trends and economic factors. They can provide financial analysis for investment options, examining the probable risks and benefits of a project or property.

Underwriter for Mortgages

To discover whether borrowers are qualified for a mortgage, mortgage underwriters analyze loan applications. On behalf of financial institutions like banks and credit unions, they review financial records and credit histories to determine the borrower's potential to repay the loan.

Analyst for Real Estate Investments

A real estate investment analyst analyzes financial statements, market research, and projections to prepare properties for underwriting. With this information, they assess risks and make ideas to probable investors.

Property Valuer

Real estate appraisers are crucial in determining the value of properties that are being sold, bought, or refinanced. They employ a variety of techniques and market trends to assess a property's worth, and their work necessitates constant learning about real estate laws, tax advantages, industry standards, and more.

Officer for Real Estate Loans and Mortgage Loans

To determine the loan amount and interest rate a buyer would obtain from a lender, a mortgage loan officer evaluates the client's creditworthiness and financial history. They also assist consumers to refinance current loans or get loans for real estate purchases.

Investment banker specializing in real estate

A real estate investment banker assists clients with debt and equity financing, mergers and acquisitions, and other financial transactions regarding real estate investments.Typically, these customers are full enterprises.

Asset Manager for Real Estate

For the interest of an investor or company, a real estate asset manager manages and maximizes the value of a portfolio of properties.14 They design strategies to improve revenue and minimize expenditures, keep an eye on operations, and handle maintenance and additions.

A Comprehensive Guide to Financing Real Estate What, How, and Why

Real estate investment is one of the finest strategies to attain financial success in life. After all, 90% of billionaires earned their money from real estate investments, as billionaire Andrew Carnegie—the creator of the American steel industry—once succinctly stated. Therefore, to remain ahead of the game,you need to have a clear mind if you are purchasing property only to earn a profit or whether you want to rent it out or sell it for a larger price. To maximize your future profits, you need also to become adept in the highs and lows of real estate financing and acquire an analytical knowledge of the industry.

The 101 Guide to Real Estate Investing in Financing

Investors may earn financially from real estate financing in numerous ways, including cash flow, home appreciation, and other tax advantages. Real estate is still the most popular investment option among investors today since it is viewed as a dependable alternative.To thrive in both the residential and commercial real estate business sectors, you must, however, approach real estate investment carefully considering the present position of the Indian economy. Let's analyze some of the main possibilities for loans and money for real estate investment.

Understanding Financing for Real Estate

A range of financial solutions are referred to as real estate financing by potential investors to acquire their capital investment. Therefore, it involves long-term financial measures utilized to obtain financing while acquiring and repairing property from outside sources. Both persons who lend money and those who take out a loan to sustain themselves financially are answerable for the process of borrowing and lending money.

Real estate investment alternatives

Purchasing a house is a costly and laborious process. There are several real estate investment opportunities, but the best solutions are to acquire real estate via bank loans or to invest in REITs. Some of the options are as follows. main sources include commercial banks, cooperative savings banks, savings and loan organizations, and banks that offer life insurance. Aside from financial intermediaries like mortgage bankers and brokers, other possible sources of investment possibilities include credit unions, finance corporations, pension funds, individual investors, foreign funds, real estate investment trusts, and the Farmers Home Administration. There's also the Secondary Mortgage Market, which provides beneficial financial prospects.

Let's give a handful of these alternatives some serious thought.

Bank Advances

Among the most popular selections among potential investors are these. It's customary to take out a bank loan and return it in installments. One of the major advantages of taking out a loan to purchase a property is that the buyer will gain substantially as the EMI will continue to fall as the asset's value improves. Moreover, a small 20 percent down payment is adequate to acquire real estate, and the loan is repaid over a generous 20 years. Low-interest rates and processing expenses, interest on the daily declining amount, interest discount for female borrowers, no prepayment penalties, and the option to utilize house loans as an overdraft are a few more typical benefits of home loans.

However, borrowers must be aware of the numerous real estate financing investing possibilities. The investment's success could be harmed by choosing the improper sort of loan. Before contacting a lender, make sure you know the requirements of each sort of loan and have a thorough idea of how the various possibilities function. **Hard money loans, home equity loans, and standard bank loans** are the three most prevalent loan sorts for investment real estate.

Trusts for Real Estate Investments (REITs)

These are real estate-related securities that are listed on a stock exchange and are arranged similarly to mutual funds,and then traded there. REITs are considered viable investment possibilities that may deliver considerable gains over time. The option to invest in Grade A commercial real estate via REITs is one of their largest perks; it increases one's investment portfolio. Additionally, as an Alternate Funding Mechanism (AIF), REITs offer liquidity to investors and are, therefore, considered as a dependable investment option.

Investment In Real Estate at a Fraction

This option is rapidly building up pace in India, after being popular in Europe and the US. This is a revolutionary technique for investing in commercial real estate, implying the shared ownership of an asset by numerous investors. A potential investor may register on the site and invest in any of the stated current possibilities,irrespective of the enormous ticket amounts. This technique raises the odds of producing a monthly rental income by opening up innovative investment options in fractions of premium commercial buildings. Considering the high cost of tickets, fractional real estate investing is a good possibility for consumer investors with limited access to CRE. Additionally, it provides an opportunity for investments across several areas and assets. Thus, portfolio risks are also minimized by diversification. The usefulness of financing for real estate and the reasons you should consider it..

• **The CAGR for real estate financing is at least 30%. Every 2.5 years, at this rate, the business doubles and the profit climbs.**

• **Interest rates decline with a nation's degree of development (the majority of developed economies have sub-1% or even negative interest rates). Therefore, this is the best opportunity to invest in real estate with extremely advantageous financing options.**

•Home finance providers have smaller net non-performing assets (NPAs) than the banking sector.

•The housing finance industry is predicted to expand at the quickest pace owing to the demand for affordable houses, followed by commerce, services, and technology. Because investors will surely obtain three times the amount compared to their house financing loan with a 20-year duration, it also provides constant income.

•A significant trend toward Grade A office space is being witnessed in commercial real estate, which has also emerged as a resilient sector. The leasing of coworking spaces is also predicted to witness a good growth in investment.

Important lessons learned

First off, a large sum of money is not necessary.

There's a prevalent notion that investing in real estate involves a substantial initial investment. Knowing the different real estate financing possibilities available to fund ventures is vital to making informed investment selections. The way you fund a specific transaction has a major influence on how the investment ends, so understanding the financial side of things is vital. Keep in mind that each real estate finance investment option has benefits and drawbacks of its own, and the ideal financing plan will vary based on the circumstances and the style of the property. It's also crucial to remember that what fits you the best might not be the optimal option for someone else. Therefore, the real estate financing decision needs to function effectively with the firm strategy. Spend some time studying the simplest investments to make.

Smaller markets are more lucrative and involve less risk.

Novice investors need to bear in mind that real estate risk diminishes with market size. Because smaller markets are confined to restricted geographic regions, experienced investors frequently shun them. This propensity provides additional chances for discerning rookie investors. In addition, compared to metropolitan regions, the ratio of the purchase price to the rent differs greatly in local markets. Renting and investing both have greater opportunities as a consequence.

Technology rescued early saves time

When it comes to real estate, being a tech-savvy investor may lead you anywhere. Understanding the most current technological innovations in the field of rent collection, which have made interactions between the landlord and the tenants easier to track, is vital in the fast-changing real estate market. For example, landlord software promotes more effective property administration. Technology also saves money and time, giving you up to focus on other parts of the property.

Finally

In the future years, there is likely to be a growth in the demand for real estate owing to migration seeking jobs in Kolkata and other major cities. It has become typical for individuals to possess small flats for both personal and financial purposes. By 2025, it is projected that the market for real estate financing will develop dramatically. Additionally, since the ratio of defaulters is large, it makes sense for genuine real estate operators to entice customers by finishing projects on time and increasing their market reach. Last but not least, if you're a beginner investor, bear in mind that all investors must ultimately overcome financial barriers as they are an essential part of the real estate investment process. Thus, begin imagining, arranging, and developing a better future if you want to integrate real estate financing into your investment portfolio!

Is it viable to buy a property without any funds?

If you wish to acquire a property without any money, you might consider about the following options:

★ Take out a loan.

★ The owner offers the property for rent with a buyback option.

★ If you presently hold property, trade it for another.

★ **Merge mortgages and offer the seller cash at closing instead of squandering your finances.**

How much should I save for the future?

It is doable to acquire your desired house at a young age. With a modest 12% monthly return, you may start small and spend $15,000 per month in SIP to build up a sizable portfolio of $12.40 in just 5 years.

Which apartment in the world is the priciest?

Located right in the heart of London, One Hyde Park is one of the world's most expensive residential skyscrapers. Penthouse D, valued at 237 million USD, is among the most costly houses. Although the penthouse is unoccupied, the building offers several features, including an ozone swimming pool.

The financial arrangement of a property development

Creating a real estate development is like creating a brand-new firm from the bottom up. It's not the same as purchasing an immediately rewarding stock on the stock market or even a completed house with a renter and revenue stream already in place.

Investing a substantial amount of money to acquire land, build the property, and then maintain it until stability is essential while growing a commercial real estate venture. This may be an extremely time-consuming and risky task, depending on the size of the site, the complexity of the development, how speculative the building is, and many other issues. To finance the project, developers require sources of loan and equity investment that can accept this degree of risk.

This section will go over the different loan and equity alternatives available for creating a commercial real estate project, as well as the pros and downsides of each sort of finance.

The stack of capital

Debt and equity are the two basic sources of private investment accessible to developers. Typically, a lender—such as a bank or another institutional investor—provides the loan. Any variety of institutions, including huge businesses, private family offices, and even individuals, may contribute stock. There are subcategories of debt and equity within each category, such as senior or mezzanine capital for debt. Preferred and regular equity may be joined to generate equity. These subcategories will be briefly explored below.

The words **"capital stack"** refer to the entire amount of funding available for commercial real estate development. This indicates the relative significance of each source of money as well as the quantity of each kind delivered. The capital stack is depicted visually in the figure below.

Real Estate Finance

Capital Stack, Debt vs. Equity in a Real Estate Development's Financial Structure

The percentage split between the different kinds of capital is often fairly varied and not every project will have every sort of capital involved, hence the data presented above should be used solely for a conceptual understanding of the capital stack. Other types of finance, such as subsidies from the government, might also be included in the capital stack for particular projects.

Both the level of risk associated with each kind of capital and its order of precedence in the capital stack run from bottom to top. Of all the capital kinds, senior debt has the highest priority of cash flows, while ordinary stock has the lowest priority. The anticipated return is the reverse of the cash flow priority.

Senior debt has a predetermined or variable interest rate, but the lender's profit is only authorized to pay the interest rate. Comparatively speaking, common stock has practically endless potential for return. Every level of capital, from senior mortgage debt to junior mortgage debt, and so on, has a bigger risk and probable profit. As you can see, commercial real estate financing follows the fundamental premise of risk vs. return. The capital providers with the lowest risk exposure have a constrained return as well.

The numerous kinds of financing

senior mortgage debt

Most of the finance for commercial real estate developments is normally given by institutional lenders, such as pension funds or big banks, via senior mortgage loans. The funds are subject to an interest rate charge from the lender, which may take the form of a fixed or variable rate. The senior lender is providing 60% of the capital necessary for the project's development in the capital stack indicated above. Remember that most projects will have a varied % balance between the various capital classes and that these percentages are merely designed to serve as samples. Senior debt is protected by a deed of trust over the property, so if the owner or sponsor fails to keep the loan in good standing, the lender may foreclose and claim control of the asset. To collect as much of their money as possible, the lender may regain the title of the property and sell it or the loan, thus lowering the senior lender's risk exposure.

Debt from junior mortgages

A junior mortgage debt is simply a smaller loan that is positioned higher in the capital stack than a senior loan. Junior mortgage debt will be present in certain projects but not in others.The basic contrast between junior and senior mortgage debt is that the former charges a bit higher interest rate on the capital given, while the latter has a smaller priority on cash flows than the former (but still has a bigger antecedent than equity).Instead of a junior mortgage loan, the capital above the senior loan will frequently take the form of mezzanine debt or preferred equity, but both have the same function of filling the gap between the required amount of common equity and the amount of debt provided by the senior lender.

Mezzanine financing

Mezzanine finance may be either sort of capital or both, and it is positioned between debt and equity capital in the capital stack. Mezzanine financing for a property has a higher interest rate than a senior mortgage loan if it is structured more like a form of debt similar to that of the junior mortgage debt.

Preferred equity interests are one conceivable structure if it is arranged as equity, Compared to a senior lender, mezzanine financing has a lower priority for cash flows and fewer rights to foreclosure. Mezzanine lenders and senior mortgage lenders sign "Intercreditor Agreements," which describe the alternatives accessible to the mezzanine lender in the event of a borrower default.

Preferential Stock

Preferred equity is a specific sort of financing that combines features of debt and equity. Preferred equity generally shares in the upside of the property's returns and has a specified rate of return.

For example, the preferred equity agreement may require the preferred equity provider to obtain a 7% return before any cash flow is provided to the ordinary shareholders. After the property hits the minimum 7% rate of return, the preferred equity holder will be entitled to a portion of any upside.

Common stock

In the capital stack, common equity is the last position. Typically, a General Partner and one or more Limited Partners contribute common shares.

In a project, the General Partner (GP) is an active partner that supervises the day-to-day operations of the development, including property selection and acquisition, development, and construction, lease-up (or sale), and post-development property management. The Limited Partner(s), commonly referred to as "LPs," are generally project investors that take a passive role.

Common stock is the riskiest portion of the capital stack since, as was previously mentioned, it is the last in line for cash flow. But if the venture is successful, it may also be the most lucrative, with practically endless return possibilities.

Debt to equity comparison

When selecting how to structure the capital stack for a commercial real estate development, numerous aspects must be taken into consideration. In practice, not all of the financing possibilities described above are available in most projects.

It is normal for a project to consist solely of senior debt and common equity, with the option of mezzanine capital as well. Every project will have a unique structure that should be decided by the parties involved as well as the project's special attributes. Which form of finance is ideal for a specific project will also be significantly affected by the terms and conditions of each funding source.

Because the general partner does not have enough equity capital or because they wish to put additional leverage on the project to gain a larger return, the project's owners/sponsors commonly elect to seek money in the middle of the stack, such as mezzanine or preferred equity. Higher leverage, however, has the potential to heighten default risk and eventually erase any equity component.Structuring the capital stack should be based on a complete study of the project, the parties, the market, and the risk tolerances of all players. Furthermore, it is vital to have a complete grasp of the strategic role that each source of finance may play in the project's success.

Chapter 2

A Debt Instrument

What Is It?

Any financial instrument used to raise cash is termed a debt instrument. It is a formal, legally binding agreement whereby one party borrows money from another, with the conditions of repayment defined in the agreement. Most feature interest, a payment schedule, and, if there is a maturity date, a term to maturity. Some are backed by collateral.A debt instrument is any form of instrument that is usually classed as debt. One technique that an organization may employ to generate cash is a debt instrument.Companies may be fairly versatile in the debt instruments they utilize and how they arrange them.

Recognizing Debt Instruments

A debt instrument is any form of instrument that is usually classed as debt. Term debt, credit, or other revolving debt—credit instruments that you may draw on at any time—with contractually fixed repayment periods are widely utilized. Debt instruments include bonds, credit cards, credit lines, and loans. Usually, a debt instrument centers on debt capital created by public and private enterprises as well as governments. The numerous kinds of debt securities that these companies issue have quite distinct issuance markets. One method to access finances is via credit cards and credit lines. Typically, these revolving credit lines have a single lender and a basic structure. Additionally, they are typically not tied to a primary or secondary securitization market. Advanced contract structure, many lenders, and investors who often participate via a regulated marketplace are all engaged in increasingly complex debt arrangements.

Debt Instrument Types

Debt has a predetermined payback schedule, which makes it a popular choice for collecting finances. Because there is less risk for both the borrower and the lender, interest payments may be decreased. A more complicated debt instrument with extra structure is a debt security. A company is frequently categorized as employing debt security instruments if it organizes its debt to obtain money from various lenders or investors via a regulated market. Because they are meant to be issued to numerous investors, they are complex.

Typical debt security tools include the following:

> ★ U.S. Treasury Notes
>
> ★ Bonds issued by municipalities
>
> ★ Corporate Debt Securities

These debt security mechanisms make it feasible to obtain money from different investors. They could have long-term or short-term maturities incorporated into their structure. Securities with short-term debt are closed and investors are compensated within a year. Investors in long-term debt instruments must receive payments for longer than a year.

U.S. Treasury securities

Treasury bonds are offered in several yield curve-denoted forms. Three main forms of debt security instruments are issued by the US Treasury: notes, bonds, and bills. The maturities of Treasury notes vary from a few days to 52 weeks. There are numerous maturities available for Treasury notes, two, three, five, seven, and 10 years. The maturities of Treasury bonds are 20 or 30 years. The American government is generating money to support itself via each of these transactions, which are debt security instruments.

Municipal Bonds

State and local governments may issue municipal bonds as a type of debt security to pay for infrastructure projects. Investors in municipal bond instruments are largely mutual funds and other institutional investors.

Corporate Debt Securities

One form of debt security product used to raise money from investors is corporate bonds. The interest rate of corporate bonds is determined by their varying maturities.Generally speaking, mutual funds are among the most well-known investors in corporate bonds.Retail investors, however, may also be able to acquire corporate bonds via their broker provided they have a brokerage account.Corporate bonds also have an active secondary market that ordinary and institutional investors may access.

Structured Debt Security Products as an Alternative Financial institutions generally utilize the various differently constructed debt security solutions available on the market as debt security instruments. A collection of assets supplied as loan security is part of these offerings. To raise funds while segregating the assets, financial organizations and agencies may choose to combine things from their balance sheet, such as debt, into a single security.

A Debt Instrument: What Is It?

To raise money, a debt instrument is employed. It comprises a legally binding agreement whereby an organization borrows money from a lender and agrees to pay it back in conformity with the terms stipulated in the agreement.

A Debt Security: What Is It?

A debt security is a form of financial instrument that has a more sophisticated structure. The borrower may utilize a regulated market to receive financing from several lenders.

What Are Treasury Bonds?

Treasury bonds are issued by the US government as a way of generating money. They are offered with 20 or 30-year maturities. Additionally, the government creates Treasury notes with maturities of two, three, five, seven, or ten years, as well as Treasury bills with maturities ranging from a few days to 52 weeks. They're all instruments of debt.

Summary

Any sort of debt used to produce money for governments and corporations is referred to as a debt instrument. Although there are many different forms of debt instruments, loans, bonds, and credit products are the most widely employed. Everyone has unique conditions for repayment, which are generally detailed in a contract.

Debt Financing: What Is It?

Debt financing is the process by which a firm sells debt instruments to individual and/or institutional investors to obtain money for working capital or capital expenditures. The persons or organizations who lend the money become creditors in return for a promise that the principal and interest will be paid back. Issuing shares via an initial public offering is an alternative technique of acquiring money in the debt markets; this is known as equity financing.

Debt financing arises when a firm raises money by selling debt instruments to investors. The antithesis of equity finance, which includes issuing shares to raise funds, is debt financing.When a firm sells fixed-income securities like bonds, bills, or notes, it is participating in debt financing.Debt financing involves repayment, in contrast to equity financing, which grants the lenders shares.Particularly small and new enterprises rely on debt financing to acquire the resources essential for development.

Debt financing is the process by which a firm raises funds by giving investors debt instruments.

The Process of Debt Financing

A firm may raise cash in one of three ways: by selling shares, taking on debt, or employing a mix of the two. An ownership interest in the firm is represented by equity. It is not reimbursed, but it does give the shareholder a claim to future earnings. Equity investors are the last to be compensated if the business files for bankruptcy.A corporation could choose debt financing to receive the money it needs to grow and expand by selling investors fixed-income instruments like bonds, bills, or notes. A company that sells bonds to obtain debt funding from investors is referred to as a lender. These lenders may be either retail or institutional investors. At a future date that has been determined, the principal amount of the investment loan must be repaid. Lenders have a higher claim than shareholders on any liquidated assets if the business files for bankruptcy.

Expense of Debt

A corporation's capital structure consists of both debt and equity. The cost of equity is the dividend payments to shareholders, whereas the cost of debt is the interest payment to bondholders. A corporation that issues debt gives two promises to its bondholders: it will restore the principal amount and ensure that the bondholders receive annual interest payments, generally known as coupon payments. The cost of borrowing for the issuer is represented in the interest rate paid on these debt instruments.A company's cost of capital is the sum of its debt and equity financing charges. The least amount of return on capital that a corporation needs to create to placate its creditors, shareholders, and other capital providers is known as the cost of capital. Investment decisions made by a firm for new initiatives and operations should always result in earnings greater than the cost of capital. A corporation is not producing a profit for its investors if the returns on its capital expenditures are less than its cost of capital. Under these conditions, the company may need to evaluate and reorganize its capital structure.

The following is the computation for debt financing costs:

Interest Expense x (1 - Tax Rate) equals KD.

where the cost of debt (KD)

The interest expense is determined on an after-tax basis to make it more equivalent to the cost of equity as stock gains are taxed, even though the interest on the loan is typically tax deductible.

Assessing Debt Acquiring

The debt-to-equity ratio (D/E) is one metric used to measure and estimate how much of a company's capital is being supported by debt. For instance, the D/E ratio is $2 billion / $10 billion = 1/5, or 20%, if the whole debt is $2 billion and the entire equity owned by investors is $10 billion. This shows that there is $5 in equity for every $1 in borrowed funding. While some industries are more tolerant of debt than others, in general, a low D/E ratio is preferable to a high one. The balance sheet statement reflects both debt and equity. A low debt-to-earnings ratio is typically perceived favorably by creditors and may make it more possible for a corporation to acquire funding in the future.

Finance for Debt versus Interest Rates

While some debt investors merely want their money secured, others also want to generate income. Market rates and the borrower's creditworthiness determine the interest rate. greater interest rates come with a bigger degree of risk as they represent a higher possibility of default. A rise in interest rates assists in making up for the increased risk to the borrower. Debt financing frequently implies severe financial performance standards that the borrower must satisfy in addition to paying interest. We term these instructions *"covenants."* Getting debt funding may be tricky. Nonetheless, it provides funding at lower rates than equity financing for a huge number of enterprises, particularly at periods when interest rates are historically low. The fact that debt interest is tax deductible is an additional advantage of debt financing. However, taking on excessive debt may increase the cost of capital, which decreases the company's present worth.

Comparing Debt and Equity Financing

Debt and equity financing differ largely in that the former delivers extra operational cash with no return restrictions. Although the corporation does not have to give up ownership to get finance, debt financing must be paid back. The majority of enterprises mix loan and equity investment. Organizations may select debt, equity, or a mix of the two financing alternatives depending on variables like ease of access to money, cash flow, and the relevance of preserving ownership control. The D/E ratio reflects the percentage of financing that comes from debt as opposed to equity. A comparably low D/E ratio is frequently perceived favorably by creditors, which is good for the firm should it ever need to seek further debt capital.

Benefits and Drawbacks of Debt Financing

One advantage of debt financing is that it makes it conceivable for a firm to expand quicker than it otherwise might by leveraging a small amount of cash into a much greater quantity. The fact that loan payments are generally tax deductible is a bonus. Furthermore, unlike with equity financing, the firm does not have to give up any ownership control. Because equity financing is a higher risk to the investor than debt financing is to the lender, debt financing is usually less costly than equity financing. The fundamental problem of debt financing is that interest payments to lenders must be paid, resulting in a payment amount that is larger than the amount borrowed. Regardless of corporate profits, loan payments are necessary, and this may be particularly difficult for smaller or newly started firms that do not yet have a regular cash flow.

Benefits of taking out debt

With debt financing, a corporation may employ a small amount of capital to produce growth.

★ In general, debt payments are tax deductible.

★ A firm preserves total ownership and control.

★ Usually, debt financing is less costly than equity financing.

★ Negative implications of debt financing

★ Lenders require interest to be paid.

★ Debt payments are payable regardless of how much money the business produces.

★ Debt financing presents a risk for organizations with unpredictable cash flows.

What People need to know about Debt Financing

What Kinds of Debt Financing Exist?

Bank loans, personal loans from friends and family, government-backed loans (including SBA loans), credit card loans, mortgages, lines of credit, and equipment loans are all instances of debt financing.

What Kinds of Debt Financing Are There?

Installment, revolving, and cash-flow loans are three forms of debt financing.Installment loans involve monthly payments and fixed terms of repayment. The complete loan amount is paid back in one single installment upfront. Loans with and without security are available. Revolving loans allow borrowers access to a continuous credit line that they may use, repay, and renew. Revolving loans are demonstrated by credit cards.With cash flow loans, the lender makes one huge payment all at once. Loan payments are paid by the borrower's income, which was utilized to acquire the loan. Cash-flow loans include, for example, invoice financing and merchant cash advances.

Debt Financing: Is It a Loan?

Indeed, the most common method to finance debt is via loans.

Is it Good or Bad for Financing Debt?

Debt financing has benefits and downsides. Debt is a wise decision for a corporation if it can be utilized to accelerate growth. The firm must, however, be assured that it can satisfy its financial duties to creditors. When deciding the sort of financing to pursue, a corporation has to examine its cost of capital.

The Final Word

Most firms will require loan finance in some way. Companies may invest in the resources they need to grow with the aid of greater money. Obtaining money is especially vital for small and beginning enterprises to acquire items, machinery, supplies, equipment, and real estate. The borrower's major issue when it comes to debt financing is making sure they have adequate cash flow to satisfy their loan's principle and interest obligations.

Definition of Loan Structure

For numerous reasons, companies borrow money from banks and other financial entities. For example, businesses might seek extra working capital to acquire new equipment, pursue development plans, buy out another firm, or pay unanticipated expenditures. The term of the loan is the period during which the borrower repays the loan plus interest. The components of a loan, including its purpose, amount, sort, interest rate, payback term, and repayment procedure, are referred to as its loan structure. In addition to risk mitigation measures, the structure might also incorporate covenants or the necessity for a guarantor. The structure is decided by the loan's aim, the borrower's risk profile, and the duration of the repayment schedule, among other factors. A loan application won't be granted unless all loan terms are satisfactory to the lender and the borrower, and the loan structure enables the borrowers to accomplish the stated objective.

Important Takeaways

The terms, interest rate, risk, collateral, and repayment are collectively referred to as the loan structure.To defend the lender against losses arising from the borrower's nonpayment of the debt, interest, and fees, the loan structure is developed to fulfill the financial demands of the borrower.

In addition to being financially beneficial, well-structured loans may save lenders and borrowers time and aggravation. A properly designed loan structure helps lenders as well as borrowers.

A Loan's Structure and Its Considerations

The key factors in loan structuring are the loan product (conventional, government, or jumbo), its type (fixed or adjustable), its amount, its length, its closing charges, its collateral, its interest rate, and its repayment plan.

Principal Amount of the Loan

The loan amount is the most significant component of the agreement as it has to be both fair and enough to fit the borrower's requests. Since different loan products may have variable fees and interest rates, selecting the correct one could help the borrower save money.

Duration of Loan

The interval between a loan's origination and maturity date is known as its term. If the funds are to be used for emergencies, one-time costs, investments in expansion, or other long-term corporate goals, borrowers must decide on maturity.

Rate of interest

Interest rates are impacted by various elements, such as the total amount borrowed, the length of the loan repayment period, the lender, the sort of loan, the collateral, and the borrower's financial status. For instance, a borrower who has a poorer credit score will have to pay interest at a higher rate. By having a better grasp of loan charges, borrowers may make smarter choices and avoid paying excessive fees and interest.

Payback

Throughout the loan, principal and interest must be paid at preset periods. Each payment comprises a component that goes toward principal reduction on the loan and a part that pays interest fees.

Attached

A tangible object or collection of the borrower's assets presented as security for the loan is known as collateral. Do the assets belong to the lender in the case of a borrower default? Lenders should carefully consider historical and future cash flows from the major source of repayment when arranging term loans, in addition to the collateral's value.

Advantages of Sound Loan Design

There are numerous approaches to constructing a loan to fit the individual criteria of both the lender and the borrower. The purpose of the transaction may not be met by the borrower and lender owing to a loan that is not properly formed.

★ A lender's assets may be preserved, tax benefits may be acquired, and a loan can be more simply adjusted as circumstances change.

★ A well-designed loan structure helps lenders to detect and eliminate risks. Through effective risk detection and reduction, lenders may establish loan

pricing that gives appropriate profits while also benefiting

Examples of Loan Structures

For example, commercial term loans are generally issued for up to $600,000, with repayment durations ranging from one to five years and anticipated interest rates ranging from 7% to 30%. Compared to ordinary bank loans, the term loan application method is less stringent and speedier, and it may be applied for numerous reasons. Because of this, firm owners who wish to invest in a specific sector or who require ongoing operations funds might pick term loans. A loan may be used to support an expansion, renovate, acquire a business, or buy real estate.

A business line of credit is a preferable alternative for entrepreneurs searching for a flexible solution to address more urgent financial needs in the case of emergencies or cash flow difficulties. A corporate line of credit generally has a maximum value of $250,000, a maximum period of two years, and an interest rate ranging from 7% to 25%.

An Illustration of a Basic Loan Payment Calculation

You are thinking about seeking a loan of $10,000, which you would return over the next 48 months with equal monthly payments. What will your payments be if the loan has an annual interest rate of 6.5%?

Answer: By inputting values for the three known variables and computing PMT, one may establish the amount of the monthly payment. N = 48, PV = 10,000, I/Y = 6.5%/12, and PMT = $237.1

In summary

The aim of the loan, the borrower's ability to repay the loan, the cash flow, and the remaining life of the assets acquired with the loan all play a part in defining the loan structure. From the standpoint of an investor, loan structure is critical. To enhance corporate profitability, borrowers have to proactively set their loan conditions. A fair loan needs to be favorable to the lender as well as the borrower.

Chapter 3

In real estate, what is equity

You'll commonly hear the term "equity in real estate" used in the context of real estate and homeownership. However, many individuals are still ignorant of its genuine relevance. Knowing equity could be the difference between taking advantage of opportunities and not leveraging your home to the maximum degree feasible financially.We'll dissect equity in real estate in this chapter by delving in-depth into its definition, calculation, and practical uses.

In real estate, what is equity?

In its most fundamental form, equity is the value of property ownership. If you were the owner of a property and there was no outstanding mortgage, your equity would represent the total value of the home. However since most homeowners have a mortgage, their equity is equal to the value of their property minus any outstanding debt.

What Elements Influence Equity?

It's crucial to bear in mind that the market value of the property may alter based on numerous **factors:**

Trends in the Local Real Estate Market

The value of a property is substantially impacted by the local housing market. A neighborhood that is undergoing gentrification may witness a boost in property values and equity as a consequence of new buildings and better infrastructure. On the other side, a fall in the local market or bad circumstances may cause values to plummet.

Property State

Properties that have been significantly refurbished or well-maintained frequently command a higher price on the market. Updating and maintaining the home frequently boosts its attractiveness and develops equity.

Financial Aspects

Buyer demand is impacted by a broad variety of economic factors, including employment levels, interest rates, and the status of the economy generally. Rising housing expenses are frequently connected with a healthy economy, however recessions may see a fall.

Demand and Supply in the Real Estate Sector

The rules of supply and demand regulate the housing market, just as they do any other. Low supply and great demand may enhance property values, resulting in higher equity. On the other side, prices may decrease or stagnate if there is an oversupply of available houses and not enough buyers. As a consequence, equity is a dynamic figure that may rise or decrease depending on several things.

Equity Is Important in Real Estate

In the financial travels of real estate investors and homeowners, equity is vital. This is the reason it's **vital:**

Wealth Accumulation: Your net worth increases in unison with equity. Your wealth grows with the value of the property and the amount of the mortgage that you pay down.

Enhanced Borrowing Power: Homeowners with high equity are considered less dangerous by lenders. Better terms may arise from this when refinancing or seeking other sorts of loans.

Possibility of Profit: If the market is solid, homeowners with high equity have the opportunity to make a big profit when selling.

How to Raise the Equity in Your Property

It requires more than only waiting for the market to rise to build your equity. Here are a few proactive measures to **take:**

Making Higher Mortgage Payments: You may expedite the decrease of your loan debt and develop equity by even modestly raising your monthly payment.

Update or Renovate the Property: Making changes may enhance the value of a property greatly. Consider landscaping, bathroom upgrades, or kitchen makeovers.

Await Market Appreciation: In places where real estate values are increasing, even maintaining a home could contribute to a growth in equity.

Avoid Taking on More Debt: Unless it makes sense strategically, avoid taking out home equity lines of credit or second mortgages.

Making the Most of Equity

Once stock has been obtained, it may be leveraged in numerous ways:

Refinancing: Homeowners who have adequate equity could refinance their mortgage to achieve a cheaper interest rate. Home equity loans allow homeowners to borrow against their equity and are second mortgages.

Invest in More Real Estate: Equity may operate as a springboard for people who are interested in real estate investment to buy more properties.Even though using equity has many advantages, it's crucial to make cautious decisions. When you borrow against equity, you face the possibility of losing extra money—possibly even your home—if the housing market sinks or if you are unable to fulfill the repayment obligations.

In the context of real estate, equity is more than merely a phrase used to describe funds; for many, it's a sign of years of devoted labor and intelligent judgment. In terms of one's financial journey, understanding, collecting, and strategically utilizing equity may make all the difference. The changes relating to equity will alter as the real estate market changes. If you empower yourself with knowledge, you'll be able to take advantage of them.

Crucial Information About Equity and Partnerships

Because it is difficult to have all the expertise and resources necessary for a successful company, it is practically impossible to establish a wealthy organization totally on your own. Even if you may begin alone, you'll soon want to make use of skills and skill sets that are better than your own.However, you probably won't have the cash flow as a small operator to give competitive salaries. You might also require money to acquire supplies or other essentials. Even if you lack the essential resources, you do have company stock, which you may employ to achieve what you desire.However, there are perils associated with swapping shares for cash, talents, and abilities. Before you consider about taking on a partner, here are the principles of equity and partnerships.

An equity partnership: what is it?

Let's start by defining an equity partnership. An equity partnership is differentiated by the ownership of business shares by the equity partners, who also get a piece of the profits, even though partnerships may take many other forms, such as general partnerships, limited partnerships, and limited liability partnerships. Each party's rights and duties, the method for making decisions, the division of losses, and the mechanism for dissolving the partnership if one of the parties decides to do so (or in the case of a death) are all stated in the partnership agreement. The parties' talks will establish the substance of the contract. Profits may be split according to several variables, such as how much labor each partner puts into the firm how much new business each partner brings in, or a combination of these. They may also be allocated depending on the respective ownership percentages.

Benefits and downsides of stock partnerships

Both advantages and cons come with partnerships. Take the pros and negatives into thorough consideration before making a choice.

Advantages

Resource pooling: Partnerships are useful because they allow people to pool their knowledge, skills, ideas, connections in the business world, and/or financial resources for the benefit of the company's greater success. Often, there would be no other way for a business to access these resources.

Better-organized operations: It might be simple to make judgments swiftly when you're the lone one in command. The legal agreement in a partnership lays forth processes that must be followed to, which will promote better-ordered operations.

Cons

Possibility of conflict: If you haven't explored what would happen in each event that your relationship may endure, conflict is a definite possibility. Consider every worst-case circumstance. What happens if one of the partners chooses to leave? Imagine one spouse dying away. How will each duo sustain their motivation to carry out their given tasks? What happens if one partner wants to put in more time or money?

Accountability: In the absence of an LLP's legal structure, partners have individual accountability for the debts of the firm. Make sure that your

83

partnership is set up as an LLP to secure each partner's assets in the case of a lawsuit or insolvency.

Substitutes for equity partnerships

Entering stock agreements is not the only method to acquire access to the resources you need as a business. When it comes to fundraising, you have a lot of imaginative choices these days. These are a **handful:**

Crowdfunding: Crowdfunding is a wonderful alternative if you need finances. In exchange for monetary contributions, you grant contributors benefits like first access, a VIP experience, or goods like T-shirts.

Friends and family: Another source of money is loans from friends and family. In addition, friends and family may be able to supply further resources, such as their business relationships.

Barter: You may provide an exchange, of their time and abilities for free products or services if your firm produces something that your ideal partners would like.Startup founders may profit enormously from partnerships, which typically allow enterprises to achieve considerably greater success than they otherwise would have. But partnerships shouldn't be undertaken recklessly. Make sure you trust the folks you chose as partners. Consider every eventuality that might emerge and design a plan to cope with it.

Additionally, receiving legal assistance might give you an extra piece of mind if you decide on a partnership.

Real Estate Equity Partnership Structure

The success of a project may be influenced by its equity partnership structure, which is a complicated process in the complex world of real estate development. Due to the collaborative structure of these partnerships—in which investors take on stakeholder responsibilities in a venture—careful preparation is important to assure interest alignment, risk mitigation, and a clear profit path. We'll go over the critical considerations, practical models, and methods that go into building successful equity partnerships in the ever-changing real estate market in this thorough book.

Laying the Groundwork

The Fundamentals of Equity Partnerships

Essentially, an equity partnership is when investors contribute money to a real estate project in exchange for ownership holdings. Equity partnerships, as opposed to debt finance, give a sense of shared ownership where investors and developers take an active role in the venture's risks and advantages. This cooperative model establishes the framework for a partnership with shared aims and duties in addition to financial transactions.

Important Things to Keep in Mind When Creating Equity Partnerships

Interest Alignment

The alignment of interests between investors and developers is crucial to the success of an equity partnership. A strong foundation is formed by agreed goals and a unified vision. Developers have to make sure that the partnership agreement motivates both parties to work for the success of the project.

Unambiguous Models of Profit Distribution

It is vital to disperse earnings honestly. Profit-sharing systems need to be stated carefully, regardless of whether they are waterfall or preferred return models. This openness helps to allow simpler collaboration by defining expectations for developers and building investor confidence.

Strategies for Mitigating Risk

There are always hazards linked with real estate enterprises, from development delays to market fluctuations. Creating an efficient risk-reduction strategy is key to structuring equity partnerships. This might include contingency plans, ways for resolving unforeseen issues, and open lines of communication for risk assessment and management.

Departure Techniques

A well-thought-out exit strategy is vital to an equity partnership's success. When identifying exit plans, developers and investors should work together to examine possibilities such as property sales, refinancing, or other choices. All parties involved may be guaranteed a flawless transition and a pleasant ending owing to this planned planning.

What is the equity return?

How to calculate ROE to estimate the profitability of a firm

Our experts answer users' investment inquiries and offer unbiased product assessments (here's how we rank investing things). Paid non-client advertising: Our partners occasionally offer us a commission. Our opinions are our own at all times. A financial performance indicator called return on equity (ROE) demonstrates a company's profitability.The annual net income of a corporation is divided by the equity owned by its shareholders to achieve ROE. Even though it is beneficial, ROE occasionally includes inaccuracies and is influenced by dishonest accounting. Value stocks may be identified by carefully evaluating a company's fundamentals, but certain factors make it simpler to swiftly pick the wheat from the chaff. One of them is the return on equity (ROE), which measures how well a corporation produces money off of cash that has been invested.

What is the ROE, or return on equity?

A financial statistic called return on equity (ROE) reflects how much net income a corporation produces for every dollar of capital invested. It helps investors' comprehension of how successfully a firm uses its money to create a profit. To get a better knowledge of how well a business is performing compared to its competitors, investors may compare its return on equity (ROE) to the industry average.

A better ROE suggests that a corporation produces income from its shareholder stock efficiently. Poor ROE shows that the company's profits are low concerning the equity owned by its shareholders.

What fraction of ROE is rated "good"?

It varies, because corporations in particular industries have greater assets and revenues than in others, ROE varies substantially by industry. For instance, the average return on equity (ROE) for online merchants is 27.05%, according to information given by New York University. But it's merely 2.93% in the advertising industry. Astute investors seek firms with return on equity (ROE) ratios greater than those of their industry rivals.

An improving trend in ROE is also promising. JP Tremblay, a teaching professor of finance at the Daniels College of Business at the University of Denver, argues that while a company's absolute return on equity (ROE) is crucial, the change in ROE over time and the circumstances that generated the shift may be even more relevant.A company's growth rate, or the speed at which it may develop without taking on additional debt, may also be assessed utilizing the utilization of ROE.

Methods for calculating ROE

Divide a company's net annual income by the equity owned by its shareholders to obtain ROE. To acquire a percentage, multiply the quantity by 100..

Net income is the amount of money a firm earns after removing its expenses. An organization's income statement reflects its net income for the year.

The claim that shareholders have on a company's assets following the payment of its debts is known as **shareholders' equity**. On the balance sheet, the equity owned by shareholders is displayed.

An example of ROE

For instance, Facebook's net income in 2020 was predicted to be roughly $29.15 billion based on SEC filings. The total equity owned by investors was $128.29 billion.

ROE for Facebook is $29.15 billion divided by $128.29 billion, or 0.227 x 100, or 22.7%.

Accordingly, its annual net income equals roughly 22.7% of the equity held by its owners.

ROE may be detrimental. However, it does not indicate that the business's cash flow is negative. A negative ROE isn't necessarily bad, but it does require additional examination, according to Dr. Robert R. Johnson teaches finance in the Heider College of Business at Creighton University."Firms in the battle to make money on an accrual accounting basis may have a ROE that is negative but a positive cash flow," by "Jeffrey S loomis".

The DuPont Equation

One way to get more information on ROE is by dividing it down into components using a framework called the DuPont analysis. By splitting ROE into three ratios via more complex research, analysts are better able to identify a company's strengths, flaws, and opportunities for progress.

The DuPont Formula

Net profit margin, or net income divided by sales, is the first ratio. By raising the profit margin on each unit sold, a firm may improve its profits. Asset turnover, or sales divided by total assets, is the second ratio. By expanding revenues while retaining a constant quantity of total assets, a firm may enhance its asset turnover.Financial leverage, or total assets divided by shareholder equity, is the third ratio. By borrowing money and producing more money than it costs, a corporation may enhance its return on equity (ROE). ROE is raised by boosting any one of these ratios. "Two companies may have the same ROE and get there in totally separate ways. It might signify a drop in net income. A business may have an artificially high ROE if it reports both negative income and negative equity. When measuring ROE, an analyst would want to make sure that net income and shareholders' equity are positive. It may suggest uneven profitability. Suppose a firm recorded years of losses against the equity of its shareholders. A year with a high net income and relatively little shareholder equity could give a very high return on equity. Most analysts would look at the company's income history if ROE was exceptionally high. It might be an indicator of excessive debt. I have also noticed that borrowing money is one straightforward, albeit perilous, approach for a successful corporation to raise ROE. Leverage is the phrase for this. Leverage is useful when you can make more money with borrowed money than it costs you, according to Johnson. "Naturally, leverage is often referred to as a "double-edged sword" due to its ability to amplify losses in situations when you earn less—or lose more—than you pay for borrowed funds.

ROE about ROA and ROIC (return on invested capital)

Investors may learn from ROE how much money a corporation earns on each dollar of equity held by shareholders. Although it is done differently, it has significant similarities with other profitability measures such as return on invested capital or return on assets.

The return on assets (ROA) reflects the share of a business's profits that comes from fixed investments such as real estate and equipment. While ROE uses shareholders' equity as the denominator, ROA uses total assets. Otherwise, the formulae are essentially the same.

Return on invested capital (ROIC), which adds a little more complexity, is a statistic for determining the profitability of investment that also reflects how much net income (after dividend payments) a corporation earns from all of its capital, including debt and equity. ROIC is determined using net income minus dividends in the numerator and the amount of a company's debt and equity in the denominator.

Though they all approach the problem from different angles, these measurements are all used to compare and contrast firms according to how successfully their management uses their financial resources to make a profit.

ROE's limits

Even if ROE is a key financial indicator for stock investors, it doesn't always convey all the information.

For beginning enterprises, for instance, where there may be a strong need for cash but possibly limited income, it may look deceptively low. Similar to this, some acts, such as incurring excessive debt, may dramatically raise risk while inflating a company's return on equity.

One major downside of ROE is that accounting methods may be employed to purposely distort it. False assets or exaggerated earnings may improve ROE and offer the appearance that a firm is more profitable than it is.

Due to these shortcomings, a prudent investor needs to extensively assess a company's financial performance using a range of measures, including ROE.

summary

One of the most essential financial variables for stock investors seeking excellent bargains is the return on equity (ROE). It's a basic and helpful measure of a company's capacity to earn money off of the cash that has been placed into it. Although a high and constant ROE is normally desired, the industrial environment should be taken into consideration when assessing the absolute value. An increasing ROE over time is also beneficial.

Real Estate Finance

Chapter 4

What Is Real Estate Leverage and How to Use It to Your Advantage

One of the finest methods for investors to diversify their assets and develop long-term wealth is via real estate investment. After all, owning a rental property offers various benefits that make the time and effort involved worthwhile. It's not always an easy operation, however. You have to put down a significant down payment and undertake careful research, and the closing process may typically go on for some time. Fortunately, financial methods such as leveraging real estate may be advantageous. However, what is leverage in real estate and how does it assist investors? To figure it out, continue reading.

Real Estate Leverage: What Is It?

Using leverage may help investors enhance their net worth in real estate. However, what is and how does real estate leverage operate? When it comes to financing an investment property, investors should examine all of their choices.

Leverage in real estate refers to the use of borrowed money or other financial instruments to boost an investment's probable rate of return. When it comes to real estate, employing a mortgage or your salary is the easiest technique to leverage a property. However, it's not always that straightforward.

People and corporations throughout the world apply leverage tactics to boost their prospective earnings. Although there is an opportunity for high profits, this is not a guarantee. For instance, if house prices decline, investors may experience greater losses than gains. Leverage may be employed by investors in several ways to acquire real estate. If you're hunting for a strategy to fund your investment, explore these several kinds of leverage in real estate.

Real Estate Leverage Types

Regarding the different types of leverage in real estate, we are discussing the source of your borrowing. Since it's an easy procedure, investors frequently start with a mortgage to aid them in gaining leverage. Let us now review some of the most prevalent kinds of leverage that real estate investors could apply.

- ★ mortgage-loan
- ★ mortgages
- ★ HELOCs, or home equity loans
- ★ Commercial Credit
- ★ Loans for Portfolios
- ★ Individual Loans
- ★ mortgages

As previously noted, one of the most frequent kinds of leverage in real estate is a mortgage. Since most individuals employ a mortgage for their principal house, this is one of the simplest techniques that people find to leverage real estate. A bank, credit union, or even an online mortgage lender are just a few of the financial bodies from which you may receive a mortgage.

HELOCs, or home equity loans

A home equity loan, also known as a HELOC, may help you leverage one investment into numerous properties if you presently own real estate, either as

105

your residence or as a rental property. "Home equity line of credit," or HELOC, acts similarly to a credit card but utilizes your home as collateral. A home equity loan, on the other hand, acts similarly to a "second mortgage" and provides you with a specific amount to pay back over time.

Commercial Credit

Unknown to some investors, they are qualified for corporate credit cards and credit constraints. New real estate initiatives may be funded by investors utilizing business credit. For instance, you may employ a company credit card, combined with a home loan or another sort of finance, to acquire a piece of real estate altogether. Alternatively, you may use it for a down payment, upkeep, or even to build your rental business in Northern Virginia via marketing or property management.

Loans for Portfolios

Investors have the opportunity to apply for a mortgage via a portfolio lender as an alternative to regular mortgage lenders. Often, portfolio lenders are smaller financial institutions that aren't compelled to complete rigorous underwriting standards. Nevertheless, as they incur greater risk, private lenders normally have higher interest rates. However, they are easier to qualify for and could be more flexible for experienced investors.

Individual Loans

A private loan might be helpful for investors who want leverage if you have good contacts with business companions or other persons who are willing to assist you financially. You may borrow money in this case from a friend, family, business acquaintance, other real estate investor, etc. For this reason, it's vital to prepare a written loan contract to specify limitations and avoid misinterpretation.

How Can Investors Gain from Using Real Estate Leverage?

After studying about real estate leverage, you may be thinking how investors may benefit from it. These are a few of the primary advantages of utilizing real estate as collateral.

★ You Can Increase Portfolio Size More Easily

★ Make More Money from Rentals

★ Defense Against Inflation

★ expanding-the-portfolio

You Can Increase Portfolio Size More Easily

Leverage helps you to expand your portfolio more rapidly than if you had to save thousands of dollars to acquire a property completely. Rather, all you need is a down payment on the loan of your choice. Then, you may be able to utilize leverage to purchase numerous residences if you can afford the monthly payments.

Make More Money from Rentals

The majority of investors frequently pay the cost of the loan plus a percentage of their revenues by renting out their leveraged houses. For instance, transform your leveraged house into a vacation rental and charge well-off tourists for it. This makes it straightforward to pay back a loan while producing money at the same time.

Defense Against Inflation

In general, real estate is a solid inflation hedge. For instance, if you have a property loan, the predetermined amount won't rise in value even while the values around you are soaring. Consequently, you will always owe the same amount on your loan, even if the value of a dollar drops.

109

Real Estate Leverage Risks

Leveraging real estate provides various advantages, but it also entails inherent dangers. For example, **you risk losing your leveraged properties if you are unable to repay the loan.** Here's what you need to know if you want to comprehend the perils of real estate leverage.

★ property-value

★ Not All Cash Flows Will Be Positive

★ If You Can't Pay, You Might Lose Assets

★ Property Prices May Drop

Not All Cash Flows Will Be Positive

Income from a rental property is never certain, regardless of how it is funded. You also need to examine the possible dangers. What happens, for instance, if your property is unused for several months at a time? What happens if you have to decrease rental pricing to the point where you can't compete? When investing in a leveraged property, there are several factors to take into mind. Before investing, investors must design a plan and thoroughly examine suitable assets.

If You Can't Pay, You Might Lose Assets

If you are unable to meet the cost of your leveraged property, you may incur huge income losses. Or your house may be foreclosed upon if you are entirely unable to make payments. Lenders may then seek your assets if the property doesn't sell for its full cost. Foreclosure may also badly affect your credit score and make it more difficult for you to receive loans in the future.

Property Prices May Drop

In conclusion, the appreciation or depreciation of property values is dependent upon the status of the housing market. It may become difficult to make loan payments if the value of your property lowers. Regretfully, having debt above the value of your house could place investors in a terrible financial scenario.

Advice on Making the Most of Real Estate Leverage

There are various factors to consider if you want to utilize leverage to develop your rental firm. Ultimately, making a significant financial move too soon could be damaging to your career. Here are some ideas for getting the most out of real estate leverage.

★ Employ Cautious Calculations to Calculate Cash Flow

When calculating your cash flow, apply more cautious calculations. Put another way, examine your finances using high expenses and inexpensive rent.

★ Avoid Trying to Use No Down Payment

Both you and the lender are at risk when utilizing real estate as collateral without a down payment. Rather, employ a down payment to make sure you're not taking on too much debt.

★ Less Leverage Is Better When Buying Your First Properties

If you're just starting to start in real estate, try to avoid using as much leverage as possible. Instead, study the essentials with as little use as feasible.

★ Reduce Your Stress Level When Managing Properties

Property management is one of many elements of operating a rental business that requires continual attention. It may be challenging for **one landlord** to manage **multiple residences** while simultaneously managing money, employing new tenants, and monitoring lease agreements. So the work load will be much thereby leading to stress and if possible you can recruit more hands to work with you to help reduce the high level of stress.

Taking Advantage of Risk and Gain in Real Estate Investing

The purpose of real estate investing is to balance reward and risk. Various economic reasons, market situations, and an investor's risk tolerance all impact how he finds a balance between these two goals. Let's discuss them.

Minimal Risk/Minimum Gain

Often referred to as Core investments, the investor in this sector is not focused on high profits. As a consequence, while the investments give fewer returns, they are safer. These enterprises frequently focus on buy-and-hold techniques in the nicest regions with residences that don't require much maintenance. When tenants have great credit, they generally produce a stable passive income. Core assets include commercial rental buildings and housing complexes.

Minimal Risk, Moderate Gain

This investment class is sometimes referred to as Core-Plus. Even while they feature buy-and-hold methods, these investments lack the same dependability. Core-Plus specializes in properties in mediocre neighborhoods with lower-than-prime creditworthiness of tenants. There may be vacancies under specific situations.

Moderate Return with Moderate Risk

Real estate investors strive to raise the property's value in this form of investment. Perhaps the landlord wishes to make changes, or a house flipper might refurbish a property before putting it for sale. Since the investor is spending more money than the acquisition cost, the risk is bigger. Such projects may also require a loan, which enhances risk even further. The gain is generally postponed until the very end, either when the landlord may increase the rent or when the house flipper sells the property for a tidy short-term profit.

High Return at High Risk

This technique requires a big initial cost with the promise of huge returns, but there is frequently a lengthy period during which no earnings are expected while expenditures remain. For example, it may take years for ground-up innovations to give a return, but that return may be as high as 50%.

Risk Elements to Leverage Higher Returns on Real Estate Investments

Although a real estate investor's risk tolerance is still crucial, the risk factors described above are more focused on the actual real estate investment. higher investment pools may tempt investors to take on greater risk in exchange for higher profits. However, if an investor needs to borrow money to invest, they might rethink, especially if they don't have a high tolerance for risk.

Astute investors evaluate more than only the prospective return on investment. They also take into consideration their risk tolerance and the situation of the market both now and in the future.

People might be less willing to buy if housing prices are increasing. Then, rental properties might be more in demand, which is an ideal argument for real estate investors to give rentals a closer look than start-ups and flips. However, if house prices are decreasing—and it sometimes happens that home prices may trend higher in one place while falling in another—then more folks might be interested in owning a property. The market for ground-up residential homes and fix-and-flips will surge as a consequence.

Real Estate Risk Management With Potential Benefits

Before making any form of investment, a real estate investor should take into consideration two additional criteria. The downside is the first among them. There is a disadvantage to any investment. Even persons with multiple good upsides frequently have at least one disadvantage. Remember the downsides when making real estate investments.

The investor's exit strategy is the second issue to consider. If you realize a profit on your investment, or in the unlikely case that you experience a loss, how do you intend to exit the transaction? You might find yourself trapped and having to take higher losses if you don't think through your exit plan before investing.Real estate investors who are successful learn to assess all potential rewards against risk. Keep in mind don't invest more than you are willing to lose.

Strategies for Risk Management In Real Estate Investing

Any kind of investing has a certain amount of risk connected with it. Real estate investment, like any other speculative enterprise, carries many hazards. Among these hazards, certain risks may be systematically evaluated and avoided whilst others are not within the investor's control. For example, investors may prevent the risk of losing all their money in a single investment by diversifying. However, risks linked with demography and unanticipated occurrences are beyond the control of any investment. In any event, it's vital to understand the degree of risk that an investor is comfortable incurring and also discover techniques to minimize the aforementioned risk, to gain more from their investments.

In this section, we will cover the numerous dangers associated with real estate investing and how to reduce these risks to achieve excellent returns on your real estate investments. Real estate risk management is the act of assessing which hazards are there in a certain venture and then dealing with them. Real estate risk management is significant because it may assist investors and portfolio managers in limiting risk depending on their financial goals.

The aims of real estate risk management

Real estate risk management is the process of recognizing the numerous hazards that are associated with an investment and then coming up with plans and methods to deal with them. It's an essential course to take since both significant and tiny faults might have a negative economic effect on your investment. Risk management helps to minimize the risk depending on the investor's financial goals.

The three basic purposes of the risk management strategy are to prevent, control, and transfer risk. To avoid risk is to simply not participate in activities that entail too much risk; to manage risk is to have an effective strategy in place to decrease the possible risk associated with investing; and to transfer risk is to pass the risk to a third party, such as insurance.

A competent property manager will always have a strategy in place to deal with any problems on the property as quickly as possible, maintain up-to-date paperwork and records, and monitor the various tasks that are performed on the property to determine if any adjustments, maintenance, or repairs are required.

Investment risk management's significance

Once all possible risks connected with commercial real estate investment are recognized, it is straightforward to develop solutions and reduce them. Risk management may also help you uncover any flaws in the property and eradicate them one at a time to obtain higher returns once it is sold. The identification of possible hazards linked with the property is one of the primary steps in risk management. The degree of risk that you incur varies depending on the sort of property you invest in and also the tactics you apply in investing.

One of the greatest strategies to manage risk and any eventualities that may result in risk is to analyze your property first, and then manage it. Once you have discovered all possible risks, you must assess them based on the potential loss they might cause you as well as the urgency of finding solutions. By doing this, you will be able to better organize your budget and ensure cash flow.

122

Real estate investment risks and measures to mitigate them

The hazard of money when investing in real estate

A lot of individuals take on enormous loans to invest in real estate. But do you realize that funding an investment with debt enhances the risk? Yes, the quantity of debt taken on is closely associated with the risk. Interest rates change, which might result in greater financing costs—which would be unfavorable to you as an investor in both commercial and residential real estate.

Risk to liquidity when acquiring real estate

Selling a house gets tough when there isn't a continuous market, meaning there aren't enough buyers and sellers. In these instances, one needs to undersell the home or wait for a longer period, frequently up to a year, for the correct price!

123

Real estate investment risk in the market

The real estate market is cyclical, meaning that it is not a matter of if but when market circumstances will move. Supply and demand, as well as economic and financial circumstances, will all influence the profitability and success of a real estate investment at any given moment. The housing market is always changing.Because real estate is so locally oriented, one of the greatest ways to decrease risk is to diversify your assets by owning a variety of asset types in diverse areas or industries. Throughout the worldwide pandemic, retail, hotel, and office space have underperformed, but industrial real estate has done well.Maintaining a keen eye on market circumstances may also help you control risk. If the market is high, it may be a good idea to sell that asset, recapitalize the firm, or update to a newer asset to prevent obsolescence. If your real estate portfolio is not overleveraged and you have appropriate reserves, you'll have enough cash to keep your real estate investment continuing until the market improves.

Investing in real estate involves legal concerns

Litigation is a key risk that real estate investors must deal with. It is crucial to have the necessary insurance in place to aid with expenses if someone is harmed on your property or sues you for wrongful eviction, contract breach, failure to disclose a problem, or any other form of legal action.

All three risk reduction strategies apply to legal risk; some risks can be eliminated, but only to a certain degree; investors need to be aware of and keep up with the most recent local, state, and federal real estate regulations to be compliant; and ensure that any contracts, leases, loan agreements, or other underwriting procedures are drafted and reviewed by a qualified attorney.Risk transfer is employed in cases like these so that even if you've followed all the regulations, tenants, borrowers, and other real estate professionals may fight eviction or foreclosure, or take additional legal action against you as the landlord, property owner, or lender.

Errors and omissions insurance addresses problems concerning employee-client interactions and is especially beneficial if an employee goes rogue and a lawsuit is made against the employee or the real estate business. General liability insurance may assist in covering property damage claims, medical expenditures if someone is wounded on the premises, and legal fees or settlement claims in litigation.

Always maintain accurate records of all financial transactions and contact with loans, renters, and investors, and make sure you're working lawfully. This information may be used to support your position in the case of a lawsuit. If you store files or speak digitally, ensure your information is safe. Cyber-security claims are becoming more widespread. Working with operating systems to understand their data security policies and processes, and ensuring that safeguards to secure sensitive data are in place.

Real estate investing's environmental risk

Property insurance covers payments connected with property damage caused by most natural catastrophes, however, named storms may need supplemental policies or coverage, such as flood insurance or hurricane riders. Hurricanes, tornadoes, earthquakes, fires, wind damage, hail, and other natural catastrophes may all cause property damage. Litigation is another important risk that real estate investors confront. It's vital to have the necessary insurance in place to aid in paying the expenses if someone is hurt on your property or brings a lawsuit against you for carelessness.

127

The hazard of real estate investing in property management

In addition to environmental causes, there are additional possible sources of harm to your property. Some of the hazards that investors face include dealing with squatters in a foreclosed property, stealing construction equipment, breaking in and stealing copper wire, renters trashing their houses as they leave, and inadvertent damages from on-site work.Property insurance will also cover any damage caused to your property by renters or other third parties; however, whether the property is unoccupied or inhabited, consult with your insurance provider and make sure the policy offers appropriate coverage. Property insurance will only go you so far in terms of risk transfer. Investors must also control risk by maintaining the property in excellent shape. Deterioration of the property is another worry. Real estate must be maintained and enhanced throughout time to prevent any dangers from individuals visiting or inhabiting the property.

How should risk in property management be addressed?

To some degree, real estate risk cannot be removed, although it may be mitigated by transferring or managing it over time. Although there are numerous inventive approaches to decrease risk in investing, they usually fall into one of three categories:

Avoiding Risks

One of the greatest ways to reduce a hazard is to avoid it completely. For example, if you want to avoid accidental drowning claims, don't acquire a property with a pool or hot tub.

Control of Risk

Risk management is the most widely employed mitigation approach as not all dangers can be avoided. Examples of risk management include keeping up with property care before difficulties appear or having the required protections in place, such as a gate or lock surrounding a pool or hot tub.

Transfer of risk

Another strategy to protect oneself is via risk transfer, which is frequently paired with other mitigation strategies. For example, having appropriate property insurance that protects homes with pools against accidental drowning lawsuits shifts the risk from you, the property owner, to the insurance provider..

While the hazards stated above are not all potential, they are some of the more prominent ones. The greatest thing investors can do is educate themselves on possible dangers and the best strategies to minimize, avoid, or transfer such risks. While property insurance and general liability are two of the finest methods to manage risks connected with real estate, the best thing investors can do is educate themselves about possible dangers and the best strategies to minimize, avoid, or transfer those risks.

Techniques for Reducing Investment Risk In Real Estate

Increase Portfolio Diversification to Reduce Market Risk

You can't escape market shocks, but you can protect yourself by keeping an eye on the circumstances of the market and diversifying your portfolio to decrease your risk exposure. The real estate business is recognized for its ups and downs owing to the economy, inflation, and interest rates that generate

131

an imbalance of supply and demand in the market. The fact of any market is that it is continuously changing and this is going to affect the profitability and the success of real estate investment at a particular period.

Follow a Systematic Legal Process to Manage Legal Risks

Litigation is a big issue that real estate investors must handle. It's vital to have the necessary insurance in place to assist in defraying expenses if someone is wounded on your property or sues you for wrongful eviction, contract breach, failure to disclose a defect, or other legal proceedings.

It is vital to follow a thorough legal procedure when purchasing, selling, or transferring your real estate holdings. Make sure a competent attorney develops and analyzes contracts, leases, loan paperwork, and other underwriting stages. Knowing the most current local, state, and federal regulations concerning real estate can help you avoid legal hazards.

Take Into Account Fractional Ownership to Lower Liquidity Risk

Real estate is typically seen as an illiquid asset since it is not frequently readily liquidated. If the economy is facing a slump, there may not be a decent quantity of prospective purchasers accessible. In such instances, you may have to hang on to the property or under-sell the asset. However, the greatest strategy to prevent any large losses due to under-selling is by integrating fractional ownership which enables you to own a particular proportion of an asset that allows you to realize your gains by simply selling them. Fractional ownership will assure that there is no net loss completely and there are alternative options for you to satisfy your urgent financial demands, if needed.

Obtain Sufficient Property Insurance to Protect Yourself From Environmental Hazards

One of the environmental concerns linked with real estate is damage to property arising from extreme weather. Other hazards include property damage from unplanned and unexplained factors such as earthquakes, severe rainfall, fires, and other natural catastrophes. The greatest protection against environmental risk is to be an educated consumer who learns about the local geography and predicts dangers based on the historical frequency of natural catastrophes in that specific place. Since environmental dangers are unpredictable, it's also vital to have adequate property insurance to safeguard you against damages brought on by natural catastrophes.

Regularly keep an eye out for any probable concerns associated with property management.

The chance of someone breaking in, trespassers on an empty property, stolen construction equipment, renters destroying their homes before they leave, or inadvertent losses from on-site development are just a few of the hazards that investors face.

134

Environmental circumstances are not the sole cause of property loss. In addition, under certain conditions, transfer of risk is one alternative. Consequently, get appropriate property insurance that covers your position and assets if the property is destroyed by renters, trespassers, builders, etc. Experienced property managers may help you limit your risk by keeping an eye on your properties often and reacting to problems on time.

Do Extensive Research to Determine the Risk of Replacement Cost

As the market's desire for space drives lease rates higher in older buildings, it'll only be a matter of time until those lease prices justify new construction, heightening supply risk. What if a superior facility with equal rents arises, leaving your investment property obsolete? Rents may not be able to be increased, and occupancy rates may be poor.

To avoid this sort of risk, you should examine the competitors in that region concerning price and features given to forecasting any rivalry that can damage your market position. Investing in required modifications to your property to bring it up to par with the quality and caliber of facilities supplied by other rental homes in the community will also help you discourage renters and clients.Real estate is undoubtedly an excellent investment, but numerous circumstances might prove problematic and cause you financial loss. These elements might come from market circumstances, political, economic, and meteorological considerations, as well as from unanticipated occurrences. You may strategically manage your property management risk procedure either individually or with the support of property managers.

What People need to know about Real Estate Risk Management

What does real estate risk management entail?

As a tool for identifying and addressing the risks associated with a particular investment, risk management comprises due diligence on the part of the investor to account for both predictable and unpredictable risks associated with real estate investing, as well as adhering to specific techniques to manage and control the said risks.

How can risk be controlled in real estate?

There are three techniques for addressing real estate risk:

avert the risk: One strategy to avert a specific sort of foreseeable danger is to think about less risky options. To achieve this, you would need to conduct a comprehensive market investigation and appreciate the asset class and the location before making any investment decisions.

control the risk: To lower your risks, you may control them to some level. To control your risks, you need to keep an eye on your property, make necessary improvements, undertake periodic maintenance, and fulfill all regulatory requirements to the letter.

transmit the risk: To safeguard your assets and interests against unanticipated threats, it is best to pass the risk to your insurance provider. As a consequence, make sure you have adequate insurance to protect you from any possible threats.

What usual hazards come with investing in real estate?

The most prominent of the foreseeable and unforeseen risks associated with real estate is market risk, which is a consequence of variations in inflation, interest rates, and the general situation of the economy. Depending on the situation of the market, the value of your home may grow or drop.

Second, there are a range of risks linked with property, some of which may change based on the individual property. These hazards include lengthy periods of vacant area, trespasser damage, and other unforeseen threats.

Thirdly, environmental dangers also have an influence. These hazards are frequently hard to forecast and include damage caused by natural calamities like earthquakes, storms, floods, etc.

What is the objective of risk management in the profession of real estate?

It's crucial to complete your due diligence by knowing more about the asset class and industry so you can correctly analyze the various hazards and how to manage them according to your particular risk tolerance. Risk management is vital when it comes to real estate investing, and being aware of it can help you cope with expected hazards and make smarter investment choices.

Leverage's Effect on Real Estate Returns

A private investor's purpose is to uncover opportunities that maximize profits while avoiding risk. When evaluating real estate investments and their prospective returns, one essential measure to regularly examine is the level of leverage employed in the capital structure. That is, how much debt is funding the property and creating the returns? increased leverage translates into increased risk. Debt financing may improve profits when projects run as expected, but it can sometimes have the reverse impact.

Leverage's Effect on Debt and Returns

To demonstrate the impact of financing a project with 85% debt as compared to 70% debt, consider the following hypothetical scenario: a $20 million property is acquired, kept for two years, and then sold for $25 million. The cost of interest for the initial investment on both loans is 4% (we will overlook amortization for simplicity's sake). While merely $3 million is required in equity for a project funded with 85% debt, $6 million is needed for one financed with 70% debt.

85% Leverage for Acquisition; 70% Leverage for Acquisition

3,000,000 Equity <$6,000,000

$14,000,000,000 in debt

The projected cost is $20,000,000.

With a $3,000,000 investment, the property leveraged with 85% debt will yield a profit of $3,640,000, or a total return on equity of over 121%. With a $6,000,000 investment and 70% debt leverage, the property will yield a $3,880,000 profit or a 65% total return on equity.

85% Leverage for Disposition; 70% Leverage for Disposition

Net profits of $25,000,000

Interest Accrued $1,360,000 $1,120,000

The balance of debt is $17,000,000.

$6,640,000 in equity value $9,880,000

Return on Equity as a Whole: 121% 65%

On the other hand, investors utilizing 85% financial leverage would lose 79% of their invested money in the case of a modest 5% market loss, whereas those using 70% financial leverage would only lose 35%.

85% Leverage for Disposition; 70% Leverage for Disposition

Received Revenues: $19,000,000

Interest Accrued $1,360,000 $1,120,000

The balance of debt is $17,000,000.

$640,000 in equity value, $3,880,000

Equity Return as a Whole: 79%–35%

Although there was a financial loss in both circumstances, the higher-leveraged scenario reveals a bigger loss. Furthermore, a real estate enterprise backed with 70% leverage would be more durable in an economic depression and have a larger chance of earning a profit once market conditions rebound.

While investors should make sure they understand the degree of leverage applied and are adequately paid for the amount of risk, highly leveraged projects shouldn't necessarily be avoided. Investors in the 85% leveraged contract in the preceding example ought to obtain a considerably greater payoff than investors in the 70% leveraged one, all other things being equal. Additionally, before sharing the upside with the sponsor, investors should make sure they acquire the majority of the money from the sale of the property until they have achieved a reasonable return on their risk.Regretfully, there's no hard-and-fast rule that defines how much more money one should expect from a more leveraged investment than from another. Examining investment possibilities non-level-wise is the best approach to compare them. The asset's gross investment performance is all that is examined by the IRR, which excludes the noise generated by debt. A property with an internal rate of return of 10% is usually a stronger potential than a project with an 8% rate of return. Having said that, the sheer quantity of variables required in building a financial model makes it tough to analyze transactions based simply on one signal.There's also the influence of fees to consider. It is not uncommon to see sponsors boosting both their fees and influence. This shifts the odds in favor of the sponsor by moving most of the risk to the investor and most of the reward to the management. The return that an investment will earn after fees should be their major concern.The usage of high leverage also shines a light on the key skills of the project sponsor. It at least indicates that the sponsor is ready to take a higher risk with the money of their investors. That indicates investors should examine where else in their underwriting the sponsor may be assuming outsized risk. In addition, sponsors who utilize excessive leverage might be making up for a lack of investment money or they can simply be oblivious to the fact that market conditions fluctuate.To ensure they are adequately reimbursed for the degree of risk they have accepted, investors should be aware of the level of leverage applied in any real estate project and realize that a higher-leveraged scenario can suggest a more severe loss in the event of a market collapse.

Chapter 5

Developing patterns in the mortgage and commercial real estate markets

A wide range of factors, including shifts in consumer behavior, modifications in government regulation, and advancements in technology, are constantly causing the environment in which real estate finance is conducted to undergo continuous transformations. As we go forward into the year 2024, several new advancements are expected to fundamentally alter the path that the sector is headed in.

The Ascent of Real Estate Technology and the Transformation of Digital

The digital revolution has affected every industry, and the real estate financing sector is not an exception to this rule. The use of Property Technology, often known as PropTech, has brought

146

about a revolution in the business by improving workflows, increasing productivity, and increasing the level of pleasure experienced by customers. It is now possible for lenders to make more informed decisions by using artificial intelligence and big data to provide more accurate risk assessments, predictive analytics, and property evaluations. Moreover, the use of blockchain technology will result in transactions that are both more open and secure.

Sustainability and the Impact of Climate Change

Decisions concerning finance and real estate investment are becoming more and more influenced by climate change. Properties' sustainability and influence on the environment are being taken into account by lenders and investors. Green standards and regulations will undoubtedly generate new financing alternatives for structures. The trend toward sustainable real estate is also being pushed by the increased emphasis on Environmental, Social, and Governance (ESG) investing, which is pressing investors and real estate owners to disclose their ESG initiatives.

The Effects of Changing Work Patterns on Real Estate

Work patterns have dramatically altered as a consequence of the COVID-19 outbreak, with many businesses establishing remote or hybrid work arrangements. This impacts commercial real estate, notably office buildings. A component of the supply of office real estate may be eliminated or repurposed as more firms select flexible work arrangements and the necessity for traditional office spaces declines.

Cost-effectiveness The Housing Crisis

A big problem presently is home affordability, because prices and rents have soared in the previous year. The major cause of this is the persistent lack of dwellings, especially those with acceptable prices. More competitively priced houses must be developed by the company for a wider number of individuals. This needs the development of new technologies, legislative adjustments, and more affordable home production.

Real Estate and the Metaverse

The metaverse, a digital platform that has the potential to drastically modify consumer and commercial interactions, is likely to affect real estate in the future. Although it is still early, the metaverse may affect our interactions with real-world environments and promote cooperation in the workplace. In addition, real estate in the metaverse may be bought, sold, and leased, which may draw new investors to the real estate market. In summary, a mix of variables such as technology, sustainability, altering work hours, affordability concerns, and the rise of the metaverse will impact real estate financing in the future. To prosper in the changing environment, industry stakeholders need to keep up with these developments and adapt their strategies as required.

www.ingramcontent.com/pod-product-compliance
Lightning Source LLC
Chambersburg PA
CBHW071045290526
45795CB00004B/1331